Flame Tree (Page 16)

# Introduction

For the past sixteen years we have lived at Terania Creek beside one of the smaller of Australia's remaining rainforests. For almost eight of those years we were involved in the defence of the forest from logging. From a small local issue, Terania Creek became a household word in 1979 when hundreds of demonstrators moved in to stop the bulldozers and chainsaws. They won a reprieve in the form of a long and exhausting inquiry. After another series of rainforest demonstrations at nearby Mt. Nardi, the years of work by many conservationists paid off when the Wran Government of New South Wales finally made the decision to declare about 40,000 ha of rainforest in National Parks or reserves.

Our involvement in the New South Wales rainforest campaign gave us an understanding of the significance of all the Australian and world rainforests, and their role in the survival of our own race in the long term. On a more personal level, experiencing a rainforest at close quarters on a daily basis has made us intensely aware of the rights of non-human organisms to exist, regardless of their economic value.

The understanding that rainforests, and all other ecosystems, have immense value in their own right is becoming more widespread but it needs to become far more pervasive if it is to curb the current level of destruction. Even in New South Wales, where it is generally believed that the rainforests are saved, fifty percent is still unreserved and available for logging. In Queensland and Tasmania, the other great strongholds of Australian rainforest, the situation is far worse, as a frontier attitude still prevails towards unexploited lands and forests.

During the years of our efforts on behalf of the rainforests, we gradually changed our native plant nursery to a specialist nursery growing wholesale rainforest plants. We now produce thousands of rainforest plants from seed and cutting for use as reforestation trees in ex-rainforest lands, as garden plants for the east coast and as tub-plants for indoors and outdoors.

Very little cultivation information was available on rainforest plants when we first began so we have had to collect our information largely by experimentation and by consultation with other interested growers. Whilst not all rainforest plants have horticultural promise, many are of great interest for other reasons, such as their suitability for reforestation or as food sources for native birds. Plants tested for hardiness have had to cope with the severe winter frost, the hot dry spring and the humid rainy summer characteristic of our small subtropical valley.

In propagation, we have learned the hard way which seeds have a viability of only a few days, which contain hidden caterpillars devouring the seed and which are considered delicacies by mice. Collecting rainforest seed is often frustrating and time-consuming, as parent trees may not produce fruit each year or may shed their seed unexpectedly early. Some of our seeds can be collected only from droppings left by currawongs feeding on our persimmon trees. Cuttings are not such a problem because stock plants can be maintained either in the ground or in tubs.

There is far more knowledge yet to be acquired concerning rainforest plants, both in their natural habitat and in the garden. This book is intended to excite interest in these beautiful plants in the forest and in the garden, as well as an acceptance and understanding of the role they play in keeping our planet habitable.

If all the rainforests in Australia were placed together, they would form a circle only 80.3 km in radius. This constitutes roughly one-quarter of the rainforest existing two hundred years ago when the first Europeans arrived.

Not only do rainforests cover a mere 0.3% of Australia's land area, but they are widely scattered, many of them in tiny patches long distances from the nearest forest of similar type. For this reason our description of a plant's natural range does not imply continuous distribution but a series of occurrences within that area. Some rainforests are found as large blocks of several thousand hectares, such as the McPherson Ranges on the border between Queensland and New South Wales, or the uplands around Mts. Bellenden Ker and Bartle Frere in north Queensland. However, much of Australia's rainforest occurs in isolated small stands or as galleries along creeks, as in Victoria's highlands or in the interior of Cape York peninsula.

Most of the photographs in the book were taken in the north-east of New South Wales. Very few of the plants are actually restricted to that area, most of them also occurring further south, sometimes into Victoria, and also north along the Queensland coast, often as far as Cape York. Some are found in south-east Asia and further afield. There are no definite geographical boundaries between the varying types of temperate, subtropical and tropical rainforest, a fact which has for years caused considerable problems in their classification.

The text accompanying each photograph is divided into two sections. The first paragraph gives information on the appearance and natural range of the plant, plus features of particular interest such as its use by rainforest fauna.

The paragraph headed "In the garden" not only provides advice on the cultivation and propagation of each plant but also dispels some of the myths about growing rainforest plants in the garden.

Rainforest Pool with Bangalow Palms (*Archontophoenix cunninghamiana*)

*Acmena smithii*
(rheophytic race)

# Narrow-leaved Lilly-Pilly

Fierce flooding batters this small creek-side form of the more common Lilly-Pilly, twisting its branches and flattening its trunk. The new growth is shiny dark red while the summer flowers become massed fruits, ranging from pale pink to deep mauve. It occurs commonly in marginal rainforest situations from Sydney to the Windsor Tableland inland from Cairns.

**In the garden:** This is an extremely hardy plant, coping with wet (but not sour) soil, full sun or shade, cold conditions and light frost. Although tolerant of poor soils it has a healthier gloss if fertilized regularly. Out of flood reach, it grows straight and bushy from 3m to 4m. It retains its fruits for some weeks, giving rich colour in mid-winter. Heavy pruning of the plant either in a tub or in the ground encourages bright new growth. Cuttings can be struck fairly easily and fresh seed germinates in 6-8 weeks.

**Family:** *Myrtaceae*

*Alectryon coriaceus*

# Beach Alectryon

Vigorous new leaves on many rainforest plants can be quite different in appearance and habit from the mature leaves. Many species of the Sapindaceae family are noted for their very bright leaf tips. (See also pages 23 & 29) The young drooping shiny leaves on Beach Alectryon become stiff and quite dull as they age and the bronze tinge changes. It is strictly a coastal shrub, ranging in height from 1m to 6m depending on the severity of its exposure to salt winds. From Port Stephens near Newcastle to Maryborough near Fraser Island in Queensland, this remarkable plant grows on sand dunes, in littoral rainforest and on coastal swamp margins.

**In the garden:** A low bushy habit and striking red and black seeds make it a desirable plant for coastal areas where frost is not a danger. Fresh spurts of growth can be encouraged by applying fertilizer during rain. The seed germinates readily in a few weeks.

**Family:** *Sapindaceae*

*Alphitonia petriei*

## Pink Ash

The speed of growth of this beautiful pioneer tree rivals some of the faster wattles. Tall and slender if crowded, short and spreading in the open, it is a common pioneer along disturbed roadsides or in rainforest regrowth throughout Queensland and into northern New South Wales. Its broad, silver-backed leaves are rusty when young. The bark and leaves contain methyl salicylate, and if rubbed, smell like liniment. Insectivorous birds love this tree.

**In the garden:** Hardy in full sun and not fussy about soil fertility, it is an excellent garden tree even in cool southern areas. With warmth, fertilizer and plenty of water it can grow 3m in one year, giving rapid shelter without too much shade. The tiny red-brown seeds found inside the black seed-cases in autumn are as hard as sand grains and just about as difficult to germinate. Pioneer trees usually produce great quantities of long-lived seeds, a percentage of which is always ready to germinate when conditions become suitable, whether or not the tree has recently produced seed.

**Family:** *Rhamnaceae*

*Alpinia coerulea*

# Native Ginger

Native Ginger was used by Aboriginal people who ate the flesh surrounding the seeds as well as the gingery tips of the roots. They also used the broad leaves to wrap meat for cooking, and interlaced them to make shelters. It is the hardiest and most common of the Australian gingers and its clumps of 1m to 2m canes can be found in semi-shaded moist places in or near rainforest in New South Wales and Queensland. The Atherton Tableland form has a beautiful red underside to the leaves.

**In the garden:** As a lush, glossy foliage plant, Native Ginger can be grown indoors or outdoors, even in cool southern climates, but to look its best it needs humus-rich soil, shelter and plenty of water. Full sun and light frost, although tolerated, will burn the leaves. The bright blue fruits remain for months during autumn and winter and, if planted fresh, will germinate within two months. Alternatively, the rhizome can be divided to make new plants.

**Family:** *Zingiberaceae*

Photo: Alex Hans

*Amorphospermum whitei*
(formerly referred to as *Chrysophyllum pruniferum*)

# Rusty Plum

There are various chemical explanations for the brightly coloured leaf-tips seen on so many rainforest plants, because during rapid growth the plants do not develop chlorophyll. After the growth spurt, the leaves gradually become green. Rusty Plum has a large blue-black edible fruit which appears in spring or summer. The tree is not large, especially in open situations where it will rarely top 5m to 6m. It can occur in rich or poor soils in rainforest between Kempsey in New South Wales and Tallebudgera south of Brisbane.

**In the garden:** Shelter should be provided while the plant is young, with ample water and fertilizer to produce good leaf colour. It is not commonly cultivated, probably because it is both rather slow and prone to scale-insect attack while still below 2m. However it deserves growing more often because of its handsome leaves. The seed should be peeled and soaked for two or three days before sowing. Germination can take between two weeks and six months.

**Family:** *Sapotaceae*

*Amylotheca dictyophleba*

# Brush Mistletoe

The Mistletoe family contains over 900 species world-wide, all of them semi-parasitic on the stems of other plants. Many are very specific in their choice of host plants and some even grow on other mistletoes. This plant is found on many different rainforest tree species from the Illawarra region in New South Wales to northern Queensland. One of the few Mistletoes that hold their flowers upright, it attracts mistletoe birds, lorikeets and honeyeaters. The bright red globular fruits contain a sweet pulp so sticky that birds must dispose of the seed by wiping their bills on branches, where it adheres and germinates.

**In the garden:** Mistletoe is not usually cultivated as it will gradually weaken the branch and may occasionally kill an entire tree. However, it can be pruned to reduce its size. Since it is very decorative and useful to many birds, it is best not to destroy it indiscriminately. The seed can be propagated by placing it on a suitable host tree.

**Family:** *Loranthaceae*

*Anopterus macleayanus*

# Macleay Laurel

Not a laurel at all in spite of its common name, this very beautiful mountain plant has striking pinkish-red branchlets and leaf-stems. Cup-shaped white flowers, 2cm across, appear in spring and summer. A lover of cool, moist places, such as creek banks where it receives good light but no direct sun, it grows from the temperate Comboyne Plateau on the mid-north coast of New South Wales to the McPherson Ranges on the border with Queensland. From a straight, single-stemmed young plant, it develops into a sparsely-branched slender shrub or small tree of 5m to 10m.

**In the garden:** A superb plant grown in a container, it can be used inside or outside in shady situations. In the ground it requires shelter from sun, wind and frost with no risk of drying out. Soil fertility is not highly significant though it does appreciate added fertilizer and will respond with moderately rapid growth. Tip cuttings strike eventually and seed, collected in mid-winter, germinates after a wait of one to two months.

**Family:** *Escalloniaceae*

## *Archidendron grandiflorum*
(formerly *Abarema grandiflora*)

## Lace-flower Tree

A good specimen of this small tree in flower can be quite stunning. Lightly-scented flowers cover the tree like a coating of galah feathers and are visible from a great distance. Butterflies love these flowers. The vivid orange pods coil outwards to reveal shiny black seeds. Leaves are small, pinnate and lacy in effect, often deciduating for short periods. It is a relatively rare plant locally, although its natural range extends from the Hastings River south of Kempsey in New South Wales to Thursday Island north of Cape York. It can occur in most types of rainforest, often in inferior soils and in unfavourable sites.

**In the garden:** Unfortunately for such a desirable tree, seed is difficult to find and young plants do not seem to favour cultivation. No particular site can guarantee a good-looking plant but they do like an open position with some shade and plenty of water. Soil fertility is not highly significant. Seed, which can occur at almost any time, must be sown immediately.

**Family:** *Mimosaceae*

## *Archidendron muellerianum*
(formerly *Abarema muellerana*)

## Veiny Lace-flower

In spite of belonging to a genus whose Greek derivation means "chief of trees" Veiny Lace-Flower is a small tree rarely reaching 5m in height. In the same family as the wattles, it is closely related to the Albizias. Both the new growth and the unusual seed-pods are very striking and can appear at any time of the year. Within its range in northern New South Wales and southern Queensland rainforests, it is found naturally as an understorey plant. It is now most often visible as a weather-beaten tree standing in open pasture in full sun.

**In the garden:** It is hardy under trying conditions of exposure, lack of moisture and frost but it does prefer well-drained and relatively fertile soil. Growth under harsh conditions can be slow; plenty of water and fertilizer not only increase its growth markedly but produce a very handsome plant. The black shiny seeds, found when the pod dries and arches open, have a short viability. Soaked overnight and planted immediately they will germinate within a couple of weeks.

**Family:** *Mimosaceae*

Veiny Lace-Flower (description opposite)

## *Archirhodomyrtus beckleri*
(formerly *Rhodomyrtus beckleri*)

## Rose Myrtle

This plant was named after Dr. Herman Beckler, a botanist and medical officer with the ill-fated Burke and Wills expedition. He resigned soon after crossing the Darling, "from sheer cowardice" according to Burke, and survived. Rose Myrtle has a graceful weeping outline, aromatic leaves, delicate flowers and long-lasting yellow to red fruits. It can be seen around the edges of rainforests or under adjacent eucalypts, usually in the less fertile soils from Newcastle to Cairns. Very adaptable to unfavourable areas, it appears most often as a shrub of 3m to 4m.

**In the garden:** Rose Myrtle is very easy to grow in full sun or partial shade, while light frost and cool conditions do not worry it if given a chance to establish itself. Plentiful moisture and soil nutrients encourage fine foliage, but fewer flowers and fruit. As a tub or garden plant it should be grown much more extensively for its adaptability and early flowering habit. Cuttings strike quickly and seed is reliable, although slow to germinate.

**Family:** *Myrtaceae*

## *Argyrodendron actinophyllum*

## Black Booyong

This is one of the large buttressed trees of the mature rainforest canopy. Black Booyong, or Tulip Oak as it is called by timber-workers, grows in rainforest at high altitudes on rich basaltic soils from Bulahdelah, north of Newcastle to Gympie in southern Queensland. The shiny leaves are usually held in groups of seven leaflets arranged palmately, like fingers around the palm of a hand. White, bell-shaped flowers are followed by beautifully-adapted winged brown seeds. When ripe, they spiral down from the tree, drifting some distance even in the absence of wind.

**In the garden:** Although so far little known in cultivation, Black Booyong has proved hardy in cooler southern areas and will withstand moderate frosts. Additional water during dry times and fertilizer during the warmest months will produce quite rapid growth. As a container plant it looks good for long periods. Seeds germinate readily if planted while fresh.

**Family:** *Sterculiaceae*

*Arytera distylis*

# Twin-leaved Coogera

All the Coogeras in a particular area simultaneously produce eye-catching pink leaf growth during winter. In the rainforest understorey and in the open they are fairly common small trees, usually no more than 6m to 7m high. The fruits develop in summer, and have the red, black and yellow bird-attracting colours typical of the Sapindaceae family. Coastal and riverine rainforests are its favoured sites from the Richmond River in northern New South Wales to Bowen in Queensland.

**In the garden:** When young it is disappointingly slow, but the leaf-flushes are so pretty that it is worth growing in a tub for some years before planting out. It is hardy in the ground and can withstand quite harsh conditions once it is established. It needs plenty of water and nutrients particularly while below 3m. Seed should be removed from the case, soaked and sown without delay, usually germinating in three weeks.

**Family:** *Sapindaceae*

*Asplenium australasicum*

# Bird's Nest Fern

Together with the Tree Ferns, this fern is frequently pilfered from the forest and many trees are felled each year just to be relieved of their load of Bird's Nest Ferns. It grows in a great variety of sites throughout most rainforests and some adjacent open forests in Queensland and New South Wales. It is epiphytic on large trees but may also be seen on rocks on the forest floor if good light is available. As is typical of most exposed epiphytes, it is well adapted to periodic drying out, and will recover quickly after rain even if its leaves have wilted and lost their green gloss.

**In the garden:** Although able to cope with considerable hardship, it will look far superior with partial shelter and plenty of moisture in summer. Cold conditions are not a great problem if direct frost and icy winds are avoided. Grown in a tub, it will last for many years and tolerate long periods indoors. It is propagated from spores. Detailed advice on growing from spores is available in "Australian Ferns and Fern Allies" (See Bibliography).

**Family:** *Aspleniaceae*

*Austromyrtus* sp. aff. *lasioclada*

# Velvet Myrtle

The rounded leaves and furry tips of this shrub give it a soft appearance, hence its common name of Velvety Myrtle. The species name *lasioclada* also means woolly branches. It is a very pretty stream-bank plant, often hanging right over the water, and in mid-winter bears black berries attractive to fruit-eating birds. Occurring from the ranges north of the Richmond River in northern New South Wales to Nambour in Queensland, it grows mostly at high altitudes in subtropical rainforest.

**In the garden:** With its roots kept cool and moist, it is happy in shade or sun. Poor drainage is not tolerated but cold climates and even frost are not a great problem. Regular pruning, fertilizing and mulching ensure a reliably attractive shrub, either in the ground or in a container. Seed germinates in a few weeks and cuttings strike reasonably well.

**Family:** *Myrtaceae*

*Austrosteenisia blackii*
(formerly *Kunstleria blackii*,
 formerly *Lonchocarpus blacki*)

# Blood Vine

A blood-red sap oozes from the bark of the vine when damaged, hence its common name. The flowers are red, sometimes purple, but the creamy calyx gives the vine a pale fawn colour when seen draped over tall rainforest trees. The stems become very stout and woody, as it is one of the larger rainforest climbers. Slender thin-walled pods containing flat seeds can be found in autumn. Blood Vine occurs in north-eastern New South Wales and south-eastern Queensland.

**In the garden:** Blood Vine is a vigorous creeper with dense leaves. If given room and a strong support such as an existing tree, it will form a mass of attractive foliage. If left to scramble on the ground in full sun, it will act as a ground-cover. Plenty of water is the main requirement for this vine, and additional fertilizer is of value. It is best propagated from fresh seed.

**Family:** *Fabaceae*

14

*Backhousia myrtifolia*
## Grey Myrtle

The early white settlers named this shrub Ironwood or Neverbreak, because of its extremely hard tough wood, and used it for tool handles, mallets and wood screws. Children found that young stems made good bows. It was once available and recommended as a timber for construction purposes. In open situations, the foliage is very dense right to the ground. The flowers are profuse, with the calyx remaining for some time after the petals have dropped. From southern New South Wales to Fraser Island, where it is called Carrol, it favours creek-side and other sheltered pcsitions.

**In the garden:** Known for its hardiness in cool conditions, it is not difficult to cultivate. Regular watering and fertilizing will overcome its tendency to slow growth in the early stages. It has been seen in horticulture for some time as a dense shrub or small tree between 3m and 7m. Its scaly bark makes it a valuable host tree for orchids. Propagation is best from cuttings – they strike easily and flower sooner than seedlings. The seed ripens in autumn.

**Family:** *Myrtaceae*

Photo: Alex Hansa

*Baloghia inophylla*
## Scrub Bloodwood

When cut, the bark of this tree exudes a pale sap which soon changes to bright red, hence the common name of Scrub Bloodwood. A beautiful indelible paint was once collected from trees on Norfolk Island by cutting channels in the trunk and draining the sap. Unusual for a rainforest species, the timber contains so much resin it will burn when green. With its long-lasting red and green fruits, it is often visible on the edge of the rainforest, or in stony places beneath it, as a dense shrub. However, it can also reach tree size up to l5m or larger. It bears showy white flowers, usually in spring. The distribution from the Illawarra region in New South Wales to north Queensland includes outliers on Norfolk Island, Lord Howe Island and New Caledonia.

**In the garden:** In spite of its handsome appearance and adaptability to cold conditions, including southern Australia, this plant is little seen in cultivation. It is adaptable to different soil types if light shelter and plenty of water are provided. Fresh seed germinates readily but is not always present in the red capsule.

**Family:** *Euphorbiaceae*

15

*Barklya syringifolia*

# Barklya

Also known most appropriately, as the Crown of Gold Tree, this magnificent plant once occurred as a canopy tree up to 20m in the drier rainforests from Brisbane to Mackay. It is now mostly seen as a dense shrub of 5m to 7m under cultivation. The golden flowers cover the outer branches in early summer. For the rest of the year its shiny heart-shaped leaves make it an attractive evergreen shrub.

**In the garden:** It is one of the most spectacular of the rainforest trees, often flowering when only 2m high. It deserves greater popularity, especially as it can cope with cooler latitudes than its natural habitat. Though very slow at first even in good conditions with well-drained humus-rich soil and plenty of moisture, it is definitely worth persevering with. Growth can be encouraged by regular fertilizing and heavy mulching. It can tolerate full sun and is not affected by light frost but these will retard growth. When grown from scarified seed it may take ten years to flower. For this reason cuttings or air-layered plants are preferable.

**Family:** *Caesalpiniaceae*

Photo: Alex Hansa

*Brachychiton acerifolius*

# Flame Tree

Probably Australia's most widely known rainforest tree, the Flame Tree is also the least threatened. This is because its soft timber has never been in great demand, and its conspicuous flowers ensured its very early introduction into horticulture. It is now grown in many places overseas and in southern and inland areas of Australia, far outside its natural range from the Illawarra region to Cape York peninsula. It is certainly a very spectacular tree when it flowers fully, though this does not occur every year and sometimes only a single branch will flower. The leaves are dropped for a short period just before flowering.

**In the garden:** Extremely adaptable, especially once established, the Flame Tree can grow rapidly if provided with ample water, well-drained soil and adequate nutrients. If burnt by frost when young it will generally recover. The large lobed leaves give the tree an interesting appearance as a tub plant. Propagation from seed, even over twelve months old, is successful. Alternatively, cuttings can be taken or selected forms grafted on to seedlings.

**Family:** *Sterculiaceae*

*Brachychiton discolor*

## Lacebark Tree

Like the Flame Tree, Lacebark loses its leaves prior to flowering in spring or early summer. The large felty pink flowers drop soon after opening and carpet the ground below, but they are so profuse, particularly in dry years, that the tree flowers for weeks. The seeds were roasted and eaten by the Aborigines. Growing to about 20m, less in southern climates, it has a stout fibrous trunk which, also like the Flame Tree, emits a hollow sound when tapped. It is found in drier vine scrubs and rainforests, often in association with Hoop Pine (*Araucaria cunninghamii*) from the mid-north coast of New South Wales to Mackay in Queensland.

**In the garden:** Lacebark Tree is already well established as a very beautiful tree for large gardens or parks, sometimes hybridizing with Flame Tree. Although hardy in most situations and in heavy soils, it will respond to applications of fertilizer when young. Frost may damage the leaves but will not kill the tree. In winter the boat-shaped seed-cases split to reveal about twenty seeds. These seeds germinate freely, even if sown some months after collection.

**Family:** *Sterculiaceae*

## Buckinghamia celsissima
# Ivory Curl Flower

Originating in upland rainforest of north Queensland, this tree is adaptable to subtropical and warm temperate climates but diminishes in size the further south it is grown. In the tropics it reaches about 30m but in Melbourne it is a 4m to 6m shrub. Latitude does not affect its prolific and consistent flowering.

**In the garden:** For decades this tree has been popular as a hardy and spectacular street tree. Whether grown as a shrub or encouraged to become a tree by pruning of the lower branches, it has a rounded canopy of very dense foliage, flushed with red during periods of growth. Moderately fast growth can be expected if summer water is plentiful and fertilizer is given. The best-looking trees grow in full sun in well-drained soil. Propagation from cuttings is successful but slow, while seed is easy to germinate and produces plants which flower in three years. The flat brown seed should be removed from the green follicle before sowing.

**Family:** *Proteaceae*

Photo: Alex Hans

## Caldcluvia paniculosa
# Rose-leaf Marara

For a period of four weeks this tree is covered with masses of small white flowers, gradually turning red over a further three to four weeks before setting tiny red fruits lasting another month. It flourishes from the Hawkesbury River near Sydney to Eungella near Mackay, often as a tall tree in cool mountain conditions. Consequently it can be grown in cooler southern climates; indeed the leaves of young plants resemble beautifully frosted strawberry leaves.

**In the garden:** It is a rapid grower but not very tolerant of full sun or exposure when young. Plenty of water and fertilizer during peak growing periods can turn it into a very beautiful medium-sized specimen tree with a solid outline. In a container, plants look fine for short periods until they grow too tall. To propagate, cuttings can be taken and fresh seed germinates readily if allowed to dry for one week to release the minute seeds from the capsules. In the photograph (near right) the tree is shown in flower. The adjacent tree is Red Cedar (*Toona australis*).

**Family:** *Cunoniaceae*

Rose-Leaf Marara in fruit (description opposite)

*Callicoma serratifolia*

# Callicoma

Early settlers in the Sydney region used the long flexible stems of Callicoma to make wattle and daub huts, so that this species was the original "wattle" or Black Wattle of the colony. It is not related to *Acacia melanoxylon*, also sometimes called Black Wattle. Callicoma means beautiful hair, referring to the fluffy flowers appearing regularly each spring/summer, usually in profusion even on quite small plants. Rainforest watercourses on poorer soils from Braidwood in southern New South Wales to Gladstone in Queensland are favoured sites. It is a typical pioneer in disturbed areas along creeks and edges of moist warm temperate rainforest on poor soils.

**In the garden:** In sun or shade, Callicoma makes rapid growth to a maximum height of 10m, but only if plenty of water is available. Its silver-backed leaves make it very attractive, and it readily adapts to most garden conditions. Cuttings strike easily and the seed, ready in April, germinates well, especially when fresh. It is important to check that the capsule has not already released the minute seeds.

**Family:** *Cunoniaceae*

*Castanospermum australe*

# Black Bean

The name of the Genus refers to the chestnut-like seed. It was a reliable food source for the Aborigines, but only after extensive preparation to remove the toxic saponin by soaking, leaching and roasting. The unripe seed is reputed to poison stock, which prompted the clearing of much of the Black Bean-dominated riverine rainforest. Its highly figured and valuable timber has been cut from rainforests from the Bellinger River in New South Wales to Cape York peninsula. Flocks of parrots and lorikeets are attracted to the flowers in spring.

**In the garden:** With its shiny leaves, dense canopy and brilliant flowers, it is a very handsome tree, reaching 15m to 20m in cultivation. It prefers rich well-drained soil and ample moisture but is remarkably adaptable. Full sun is not a problem and light frost is tolerated. As an indoor plant, Black Bean is often grown in groups of 5 to 10 seedlings. The seedling grows rapidly up to 0.5m and slows down for a year or so before taking off again.

**Family** *Fabaceae*

*Cinnamomum oliveri*

# Oliver's Sassafras

Timber-workers call this tree Camphorwood for its fragrant timber. It is quite different in appearance from its close relative Camphor Laurel (*Cinnamomum camphora*). The latter is a serious weed tree in subtropical areas. Laurels bear fruits of high food value for pigeons as do avocadoes (also in the Laurel family) for humans but Oliver's Sassafras is rather sporadic in its fruit production. The scented leaves with wavy edges are a distinctive feature of this plant. It occurs in many highland and lowland rainforests on poor soil from the Illawarra region in New South Wales to Eungella near Mackay in Queensland.

**In the garden:** It grows into a large tree to 20m even in the open, with a beautiful crown of thick foliage. Good soil and ample water will hasten growth in the early stages, when it can be rather slow. Shelter from frost and severe exposure is appreciated. It lasts well as a tub plant indoors and outdoors. When propagating the seeds, the black flesh should be peeled off first or they will not germinate.

**Family:** *Lauraceae*

*Commersonia bartramia*

# Brown Kurrajong

Brown Kurrajong is an important tree in rainforest regeneration due both to its ability to withstand exposure and to its extremely fast growth rate of 3m per year under suitable conditions. Its filtered shade does not inhibit other plants from developing underneath. The pale trunk and the horizontally layered appearance of the foliage are very attractive. At Christmas-time, dense white flowers add the impression of snow, hence its name "Scrub Christmas Tree" in northern New South Wales. It favours rainforest regrowth from the Bellinger River in New South Wales to Cape York peninsula and Malaysia.

**In the garden:** Frost will set this small tree back when young but it is otherwise very hardy and, if given plenty of water and fertilizer, will quickly reach 7m to 8m. Propagation from cuttings is easy and produces early-flowering plants. Seed can be collected from the hairy seed-cases during summer and autumn and germinates well if treated with boiling water.

**Family:** *Sterculiaceae*

*Cordyline petiolaris*
(formerly *Cordyline fruticosa*)

# Broad-leaved Palm Lily

This elegant Palm Lily has branching spikes of tiny purple flowers, followed by edible red fruits which last for several weeks. In north-eastern New South Wales and south-eastern Queensland, it is a common plant in rainforests and adjacent open forests, wherever it can receive good light and moisture, though not necessarily in rich soil. Most specimens seen are 2m to 4m tall but some many-branched old plants reach 7m.

**In the garden:** Its adaptability in a wide range of natural conditions makes it hardy under cultivation. In temperate and tropical areas it grows best in semi-shade, with additional moisture available in dry spells and regular applications of fertilizer. Plants kept in containers remain quite short and can be taken inside for long periods. Propagation by either stem cuttings or division is successful and seed germinates reliably but may take two months.

**Family:** *Agavaceae*

Photo: David Milledg

## *Cryptocarya laevigata*
# Glossy Laurel

Glossy Laurel has been grown in glasshouses in England since the early 19th century, (from "The Encyclopaedia of Australian Plants", see Bibliography) yet it is relatively unknown in Australia. It is one of the most handsome of the rainforest shrubs, growing as an understorey plant in rich basalt or alluvial soil from northern New South Wales to Cairns in Queensland. The bright autumn fruits are not plentiful but they contrast strongly with the shiny foliage.

**In the garden:** Although preferring some shelter, and occurring naturally under the canopy in heavy shade, Glossy Laurel will tolerate full sun by arranging its leaves closer together. It is not a rapid grower and can be kept in a tub for some time, looking very decorative either indoors or out. Good nutrition and plenty of water are important but cool conditions are acceptable if it can be protected from heavy frost. Seeds are slow to germinate and cuttings take several months to establish roots.

**Family:** *Lauraceae*

## *Cupaniopsis anacardioides*
# Tuckeroo

Windswept headlands, sand dunes and littoral (coastal) rainforest are all home to this hardy and adaptable small tree. Growing to 10m in rainforest, Tuckeroo is smaller when isolated and under conditions of extreme coastal exposure will remain a dense shrub. Massed bunches of yellow fruits are produced regularly each year. Currawongs and fig birds enjoy the seeds which are exposed as the fruits ripen in early summer. It occurs from the mid-south coast of New South Wales to Queensland and the Northern Territory.

**In the garden:** Tuckeroo makes a handsome small to medium-sized shade tree for coastal areas. It has been extensively used as a street tree in Brisbane. Applications of fertilizer coupled with plenty of water will encourage growth up to 2m per year – very different from the slow growth normally attributed to this tree. Seeds will germinate in a month or so but before sowing these should be soaked to drown caterpillars and after sowing must be protected from mice.

**Family:** *Sapindaceae*

*Cuttsia viburnea*
# Native Elderberry

The alternative name, Honey Bush, is more appropriate for this plant. It is not related to the common Elderberry and is much more attractive, without its suckering habit. The sweetly-scented, starry flowers appear in profusion in late spring. It is always found in cool moist situations, usually beside creeks at high elevations. Although occurring in rainforest between the Comboyne Plateau on the mid-north coast of New South Wales and Cunningham's Gap south-west of Brisbane, it can be seen along creeks in open forest as far north as the Blackdown Tableland, inland from Rockhampton.

**In the garden:** A strong preference for cool places with no risk of dryness limits it somewhat as a garden plant. It is however suitable for some dank and difficult areas and does not mind poor soil. It is frost-hardy and fast-growing to 3m to 4m but will become leggy if not pruned, particularly when grown as a tub plant. Cuttings are successful and so are the seeds which are extremely fine. These should be sown sparsely.

**Family:** *Escalloniaceae*

*Davidsonia pruriens var. jerseyana*
# Davidson's Plum

A brilliant red pulp, rather sour but delicious when made into jam or wine, is contained in these clustered fruits. They are all coated with fine golden hairs – *pruriens* means itching. Mature trees form a clump of stems 4m to 6m high, each with a crown of striking and highly ornamental leaves. This variety of Davidson's Plum occurs only in riverine rainforest of the Brunswick and Tweed valleys on the far north coast of New South Wales. The other variety, *Davidsonia pruriens var. pruriens*, occurs in north Queensland.

**In the garden:** Davidson's Plum is not difficult to grow if given shelter from extreme frost and heat. While young it makes an interesting container plant which can eventually be planted out in a well-drained site. Regular fertilizing, mulching and watering will maintain its attractive leaves and induce fruit to set in three or four years. The fruit ripens early in the new year and the seeds are quick to germinate once the flesh is removed. The seeds should be protected from mice.

**Family:** *Davidsoniaceae*

*Dawsonia superba*

# Giant Moss

The species name "superba" means magnificent, an unlikely name for a moss, but at 10cm to 50cm this is one of the biggest mosses found anywhere in the world. Like a forest of tiny pine trees, it forms extensive colonies in shady moist places, often in heavy clay soils of low fertility such as road cuttings. In such sites it flourishes right along the east coast of mainland Australia, Tasmania and New Zealand. At certain times of the year it appears more blue than green.

**In the garden:** *Dawsonia* is rarely seen in cultivation but is easy to grow with minimal attention in shade. It does not require either fertilizer or well-drained soil but water is always appreciated and cannot be overdone. During dry periods it will wilt severely but recovers quickly with watering. The long underground stems which can tap hidden moisture also make it difficult to transplant. If grown in shallow trays of clay soil, it can be easily divided.

**Family:** *Dawsoniaceae*

*Decaspermum parviflorum*

# Silky Myrtle

This is a lovely plant throughout the year and is well named Silky Myrtle. The pink leaf tips are clothed in fine silky silver hairs even in mid-winter when there is no active growth. The flowers, although profuse, are short-lived. Small black fruits, ripe in late winter, contain roughly ten seeds. It can be a small tree to 8m but is mostly seen as a well-shaped glossy shrub 3m to 4m tall. From Gosford north of Sydney to North Queensland and further north as far as India, Silky Myrtle is usually found in drier rainforests often in stony areas with shallow soils.

**In the garden:** A very attractive shrub, Silky Myrtle is rarely without its colourful leaf tips, especially if lightly pruned and fertilized. It can be grown in full sun or light shade in well-drained soil and makes a lovely container plant which can be brought inside for short periods. Cool conditions, even light frost are not a problem. It is propagated by cutting or from fresh seed, which should be removed from the flesh prior to sowing.

**Family:** *Myrtaceae*

*Diploglottis australis*

## Native Tamarind

Native Tamarind belongs in the same family as the rambutan, lychee and longan of Asia. Its bright orange fruit is sour but juicy and pleasant to taste. Birds and fruit bats relish it and in spring the ground beneath the trees is littered with spat-out seeds, which, incidentally, are far more likely to germinate than untouched seed. The straight trunk is crowned with beautiful pinnate leaves, rusty velvet when young. From the Illawarra region in New South Wales to Proserpine near Bowen in Queensland, it grows in a wide range of rainforest habitats.

**In the garden:** If given a favourable position out of frost and wind, Native Tamarind will grow in sun or shade. It can be slow but when encouraged with frequent watering and regular fertilizer it has a splendid appearance either as a tub plant or in the ground. Seed should be planted immediately after collection when it will germinate quickly.

**Family:** *Sapindaceae*

26

*Diploglottis campbellii*

# Small-leaved Tamarind

After extensive clearing of rainforests for agriculture, only a handful of the trees which produce this delightful fruit still exist in their natural state, putting the species very high on the rare and endangered list. It is now found in only a few sites in the riverine rainforest areas of the Richmond and Tweed River valleys in northern New South Wales and at Tallebudgera south of Brisbane. Several large forest trees up to 25m are known, but in the open it is smaller and more spreading with a handsome shady crown. The juicy red fruit, actually an aril enclosing a hard woody seed, is pleasant to eat or use in drinks or jams, although it is very acid.

**In the garden:** Slow growth when young is frustrating but this tree looks attractive at all stages and flowers and fruits when quite small. Unsuitable for very cold or arid areas, it requires good drainage with high nutrient and water supplies. Sheltered sites with partial shade are preferred. The seed should be removed from the red flesh and it germinates in two to three weeks if fresh.

**Family:** *Sapindaceae*

*Ehretia acuminata*

# Koda

These yellow berries, produced in great quantities during autumn, are eaten by many birds. In spring, the sweetly-scented flowers form dense white panicles. Although recorded as a medium to large tree in the natural forest, most specimens are now seen less than 10m tall in rainforest regrowth. Koda occurs from Bega in New South Wales to Cape York in Queensland but it is not restricted to Australia, being found also in south-east Asia.

**In the garden:** Its ability to flower and fruit at an early age makes it a good choice for attracting birds to the garden. For a brief time during winter it is deciduous, hence its resistance to frost damage; for the rest of the year it grows quickly in sun or partial shade in a variety of soil types. A drawback to an otherwise splendid garden tree is its tendency when very young to be defoliated by caterpillars shortly before the leaves drop in winter. Fresh seed is very easy to germinate.

**Family:** *Boraginaceae*

*Elaeocarpus reticulatus*

# Blueberry Ash

These dainty flowers are aniseed-scented and have given Blueberry Ash alternative names such as Lily of the Valley Tree and Fairy Petticoats. In winter the brilliant blue fruits hang for months and are sought after by currawongs and bower-birds. It varies in habit from a 2m to 3m shrub to a small tree and is commonly seen in marginal rainforest areas, in moist open forest along creeks and on slopes facing the sea. Its natural range from Fraser Island in Queensland to Flinders Island in Bass Strait accounts for its hardiness in cold conditions.

**In the garden:** Incredibly tough, it is able to cope with frost, salt air, poor soil, wind, full sun and periodic dryness, though ample moisture is important when the plant is young. The pink-flowered form, Prima Donna, is outstanding, with its very compact shape and leaf edges frosted with white. Seed is slow to germinate, taking up to two years, but cuttings are reasonably easy.

**Family:** *Elaeocarpaceae*

Photo: Alex Hansa

*Elatostema reticulatum*

# Rainforest Spinach

This soft herb is also called Soft Nettle as it belongs to the nettle family, but it bears no resemblance to the stinging nettle and has no stinging hairs. The leaves and young stems are edible and can be used as a substitute for spinach. The Aborigines boiled it in bark troughs or large sea-shells. Usually about 0.3m in height, it can cover quite large areas of the forest floor adjacent to streams or in otherwise wet sites from northern New South Wales to north Queensland.

**In the garden:** It is not a colourful plant but its lush appearance makes it a most useful plant for shady positions wherever water is available. Easily propagated from cuttings, it can be used indoors. It will not tolerate frost, salt or exposure to wind.

**Family:** *Urticaceae*

*Elattostachys nervosa*

## Beetroot

Bright red new growth has given Beetroot its name. Coloured growth like this does not always occur during the main summer growing season – early spring and late autumn are good times to see brilliant leaf colour. Alternatively called Green Tamarind, it is mostly seen as a small tree under 10m in drier rainforests, though it also occurs as a larger tree in rich soil from mid-north New South Wales to Gympie in Queensland.

**In the garden:** For the best displays of new leaf colour this tree should be planted in very well-drained soil and given plenty of water and fertilizer. If kept as a tub plant for the first year, its heavily-toothed juvenile leaves can be appreciated fully. The black seeds are often absent from the pink seed capsules, but are easy to germinate when they can be found.

**Family:** *Sapindaceae*

## *Endiandra pubens*
# Hairy Walnut

This beautiful fruit, up to 6cm in diameter, looks nothing like a hairy walnut as the common name suggests. However the timber is supposed to resemble that of the European walnut, and the underside of the leaves is hairy. The fruits are produced only every two or three years and are dropped sporadically over the warmer months. Occasionally reaching 30m, it is mostly seen as a low bushy tree on rich alluvial soil from the Bellinger River in New South Wales to the central Queensland coast.

**In the garden:** Although quite slow-growing, Hairy Walnut is worth cultivating for the beautiful dense foliage with its coppery new growth. It will last for years as an attractive tub-plant and can be used indoors. A protected position with good water and soil nutrients is required. The seed may take some months to throw up a shoot but it will have already developed extensive roots so a deep container is necessary for sowing. Cuttings strike rather slowly.

**Family:** *Lauraceae*

## *Ervatamia angustisepala*
# Banana Bush

These pretty yellow fruits resemble tiny bananas but are not edible, and belong to the same family as the highly poisonous Oleander. The white windmill-shaped flowers are very sweetly scented and all parts of the plant when broken exude a white latex. When growing as an understorey shrub it is dark-leaved with open branches; in regrowth after clearing it is shorter and denser with yellow leaves. It grows in a variety of sites, from the mid-north coast of New South Wales to north Queensland.

**In the garden:** A healthy specimen grown in good light without direct sun can look very attractive when in flower or fruit. Unfortunately it is sometimes defoliated by caterpillars down to the last leaf. Possibly it would sustain less insect damage in southern areas and could be recommended for gardens. New plants can be propagated from cuttings or fresh seed.

**Family:** *Apocynaceae*

*Euodia elleryana*

# Pink Euodia

Many birds visit Euodia for the flowers in summer and for the black seeds in winter. Butterflies also are attracted to the flowers, most notably the brilliant blue Ulysses butterfly whose larvae feed on the leaves. Flowers and leaves are arranged on the outer branches, the inside of the tree being very open. Although capable of growing to 25m, Euodia is mostly found as a 7m to 10m tree which commences flowering when only two or three years old. Seen close to the coast usually in riverine rainforest, it extends naturally from the Clarence River in New South Wales to north Queensland and into Papua New Guinea.

**In the garden:** It is a very co-operative tree, being hardy, fast-growing and adaptable to such unfavourable sites as asphalt car parks. However it does not appreciate frosts. Wet soils are acceptable if they are not too heavy or sour. Plentiful water and fertilizer produce rapid growth. The seed is unpredictable, regardless of freshness, and gives germination rates varying from 0% to 100%.

**Family:** *Rutaceae*

*Eupomatia bennettii*

# Small Bolwarra

For less than one day this beautiful scented flower blooms in the low intensity light of the rainforest floor. In that time it needs to be pollinated by small beetles if it is to set seed. Each flower produces one seedcase with dozens of seeds inside. The plant is a small shrub less than 1m with only one or two slender stems, and is found in moist volcanic soils from the Nambucca valley near Coff's Harbour in New South Wales to north Queensland. This species belongs to an ancient and primitive family with only one other member, the shrub *Eupomatia laurina* or Smooth Bolwarra. So despite its modest size, it is of enormous interest to world science.

**In the garden:** It is somewhat straggly and not alluring as a garden specimen but that does not prevent it being sought after by many enthusiasts for its lovely flower. When young it sometimes appears to die back but shoots again in the spring from a tuberous root. The seed is difficult to find, as the plant is uncommon, and it germinates very slowly. Cuttings are usually successful.

**Family:** *Eupomatiaceae*

*Ficus fraseri*

# Sandpaper Fig

Of the two Sandpaper Figs this is the larger and more spreading. It varies considerably in habit from a small open-branched tree of 6m to a 15m tree with a dense round canopy. The fruits in this picture are immature – they will ripen at different stages and provide food over an extended period for fruit-eating birds, particularly fig birds. The fruits are often available for birds in spring when food is otherwise scarce. It grows from the Hunter River in New South Wales to the Atherton Tableland in Queensland.
**In the garden:** In spite of its general hardiness and attractive appearance, Sandpaper Fig has been rarely used in horticulture. It grows very rapidly, especially when grown in rich soil with plenty of moisture. In cold areas it may become semi-deciduous for a short time. Seed can be germinated easily.

**Family:** *Moraceae*

*Ficus macrophylla*

# Moreton Bay Fig

The smooth rusty underside of the leaves readily distinguishes this large fig tree. It is found in all types of coastal rainforest from the Illawarra region in New South Wales to north Queensland. Although familiar as a spreading tree in parks, in its natural habitat it behaves as a "strangler". Starting life as a fine seed dropped by birds high on the branches of another tree, it lives as an epiphyte on accumulated leaf debris and may take many years to send fine roots down to the ground. Once anchored in the soil, the roots thicken dramatically, fusing with each other to form a latticework which eventually becomes strong and continuous enough to prevent trunk expansion of the host tree. The host tree dies and decays leaving a massive hollow column of fig roots topped by a crown emergent from the rest of the rainforest canopy.
**In the garden:** It is easy to grow in the ground, omitting the epiphytic stage, but it needs plenty of room and is not suitable for small gardens. This hardy fig makes an excellent tub plant. The seed germinates readily if fresh.

**Family:** *Moraceae*

Strangling roots typical of *Ficus macrophylla* and many other large rainforest figs (description opposite)

*Flagellaria indica*

# Supple Jack
or Whip Vine

Looking very like a scrambling bamboo, this vine is commonly seen in rainforests and their margins. It is very vigorous and often appears sprouting out the top of tall trees using the very strong coiled leaf-tip for attachment. This dense flowerhead later forms white berries that attract fruit-eating birds. Flagellaria occurs along the coast from Sydney to north Queensland and in the Northern Territory. The Aborigines made a remedy for toothache, sore throat and chest complaints from the young shoots and buds. The long stems were used to make fish-traps, and as ropes to aid tree-climbing.

**In the garden:** Although large and active, it can be encouraged to climb established trees and need not take up a lot of ground space. It makes an interesting tub plant. Plenty of moisture, reasonable soil and protection from severe cold are required. It is presumably propagated from seed but we have not had experience with its germination.

**Family:** *Flagellariaceae*

*Geissois benthamii*

# Red Carabeen

Growth shoots such as this one on a young plant, occur all over the tops of Red Carabeen trees at the end of summer so that the red crowns appear from a distance to be in flower. The flowers themselves are pale-yellow, occurring in mid-summer. Each tree is large and impressive with heavy buttressing. Cool mountain situations suit it best from Taree in New South Wales to Mt. Tamborine south of Brisbane.

**In the garden:** Too large for small gardens, Red Carabeen makes a splendid park tree, able to withstand full sun and quite cold southern conditions. Rapid growth and brilliant new leaves can be encouraged with plenty of water during dry spells and regular fertilizer when young. It makes a handsome specimen plant in a container and can be used indoors if the growth tips are nipped to encourage bushiness. The thin pointed seed capsules are ripe from May to July and will open and shed their seed in a few days – they need to be watched closely. The seed germinates within three to four weeks.

**Family:** *Cunoniaceae*

34

*Glochidion ferdinandi*

# Cheese Tree

Named rather loosely for the red or yellow fruits which are supposed to resemble round cheeses, this tree grows as a pioneer on the edge of rainforest or in regenerating areas. Its thick crown of shiny leaves spreads out to form a small shade tree of 10m to 12m when grown in the open. Generally the banks of watercourses are favoured but it can be seen in harsher conditions from southern New South Wales to Carnarvon Gorge in Queensland.

**In the garden:** This tree has attractive foliage but it can be damaged by leaf miners when young and, in some districts, by leaf-tying caterpillars. Ample water and fertilizer will help the tree to recover quickly. It adapts well to different soils, tolerating full sun as well as cold conditions. Cuttings strike very quickly, these being quite different in appearance from seedlings. As there are male and female trees, seed can be difficult to obtain but it germinates readily if removed from the seed-capsule before planting.

**Family:** *Euphorbiaceae*

*Grevillea robusta*

# Silky Oak

In spring and summer large numbers of honey-eaters, noisy miners and lorikeets gather in Silky Oaks to feed on the copious nectar in the flowers. The tree's natural range from the Guy Fawkes River in New South Wales to Maryborough near Fraser Island has been considerably expanded by extensive planting. Originally a subtropical rainforest tree, its tall thin silhouette can now be seen in dry inland and cold southern areas.

**In the garden:** Silky Oak is exceptionally hardy and adapts well to a wide variety of soil conditions and moisture levels. Frost may be a problem for very young trees but full sun is quite acceptable. Growth is fast if plenty of water and soil nutrients are provided in the early stages. In Europe, its ferny pinnate leaves have made it a popular indoor plant. Seed is ready in mid-summer, it germinates well and can be stored, unlike most rainforest seed. Seedlings are often used as rootstocks for grafting other less hardy *Grevilleas*.

**Family:** *Proteaceae*

## *Harpullia alata*
# Winged Tulip

This small understorey shrub has been named alata (from the Latin *"ala"* meaning wing) because of the narrow wing along both sides of the long leaf axis. One or two thin stems support the crown of unusually long leaves. Not a common plant, Winged Tulip is found on the richer rainforest soils in mountain areas from Bulahdelah in New South Wales to Innisfail south of Cairns. The fruits are yellow with black seeds half-covered by a bright red fleshy aril. Birds eat these for the aril and regurgitate the undamaged seed.

**In the garden:** It makes an unusual, slow-growing shrub for shady places where moisture and soil fertility are high. It does not like exposure or cold. Kept in a tub, its preferred conditions can be provided and the interesting leaves easily seen. The seed germinates readily if sown immediately after collection.

**Family:** *Sapindaceae*

## *Harpullia hillii*
# Blunt-leaved Tulip

These showy seed-cases are often completely empty. The seed, when present, is large, black and shiny and almost covered by a contrasting red aril. In silhouette the tree is compact with a thick dark crown. The pinnate leaves are broad, each leaflet having a distinctive rounded notched end. The shiny new growth often has a lovely metallic blue-black lustre. Growing naturally from Kempsey in New South Wales to Ayr south-east of Townsville, it is seen mainly as a small to medium tree, rarely over 10m.

**In the garden:** Although not commonly seen in cultivation, it is worth growing for its pleasing shape and yellow fruit. It dislikes frost and severe wind but can cope with full sun if soil moisture and fertility are high. In December, seed can be collected and germinated easily.

**Family:** *Sapindaceae*

*Harpullia pendula*

# Tulipwood

Tulipwood has also been named Black Tulip for its beautiful timber, highly figured with contrasting dark and light bands. It was once a characteristic member of the drier rainforests between the Bellinger River in New South Wales and Cairns in north Queensland. It is now most often seen as an ornamental street tree, particularly in Brisbane. Generally it is under 10m in height but some older specimens are large and spreading. The orange seed-cases with their shiny black seeds mature between early winter and late spring.

**In the garden:** Although preferring rich soils, it is fairly adaptable to new sites. Protection from frost is necessary in the early stages but it is otherwise hardy even in rather dry conditions and certainly does not mind full sun. Plenty of water and fertilizer in the early stages can overcome a slight tendency to tardiness. Seed germinates well in a few weeks if it is soaked first to drown any caterpillars.

**Family:** *Sapindaceae*

*Helmholtzia glaberrima*

# Stream Lily

The dark green leaves of this beautiful lily-like plant form large clumps up to 2m high, with tall feathery white to pale pink spikes appearing in summer. It thrives in quite dense colonies amongst the rocks of creeks and in poorly drained areas in rainforest gullies. Young plants often start life on wet rocks and gain a strong enough foothold to withstand frequent inundation. It occurs only on the McPherson Ranges and in other nearby rainforests.

**In the garden:** This is an excellent landscaping plant for shady areas as it grows rapidly and always looks healthy if cool wet conditions are provided. As a rockery plant or container plant it does equally well. Propagation is easy, either by division of small clumps or from seed. The fine seed should be collected just as the capsules begin to open in May and then dried in a paper bag for a week or so before sowing. Viability is lost fairly quickly.

**Family:** *Philydraceae*

Photo: Alex Hansa

*Hicksbeachia pinnatifolia*

# Red Boppel Nut

Multiple stems, each with a crown of large, stiff, toothed leaves make this small tree easily distinguishable. Purplish flowering spikes in spring are scented and in mid-summer form strings of brilliant red nuts which cockatoos love. These nuts are said to be edible and have been eaten without ill-effect, but they do contain prussic acid. The plant grows in warmer locations, mostly on rich soil in widely separated populations in the Nambucca-Bellinger area, the Richmond and Tweed valleys and the Atherton Tableland in north Queensland.

**In the garden:** It is a very striking garden plant and is hardy once established but it does have some problems. As a seedling it is prone to fungal infections of roots and leaves as well as leaf-beetle attack which skeletonizes some leaves. One solution is to encourage fast growth up to 1m in height by giving ample water and fertilizer, coupled with excellent drainage. Frost will burn new growth and harsh exposure yellows the leaves. Seed is easy to germinate.

**Family:** *Proteaceae*

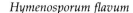

## *Hymenosporum flavum*
# Native Frangipani

In spite of the characteristic scent, this plant is not related to the exotic Frangipani. The highly perfumed and very attractive flowers are borne all over the plant in late spring and last for some weeks. Native Frangipani thrives in all rainforest types and often in open country previously occupied by rainforest. Ranging from a shrub to a tall tree, it grows naturally from Sydney to the Windsor Tableland near Cairns. Its distribution is now far greater as it has been introduced to many southern and inland areas.

**In the garden**: The toughness and adaptability of this tree have made it very successful in gardens throughout much of Australia. Surprisingly, it looks best in unfavourable situations where it is forced to stay small and bushy, usually flowering more profusely. Plenty of moisture and well-drained humus-rich soil will produce quick growth in the early stages but it can become rather leggy so pruning is advisable if a more compact plant is wanted. It withstands full sun and frost. The seed is available in late summer and germinates within a few weeks.

**Family:** *Pittosporaceae*

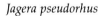

## *Jagera pseudorhus*
# Foambark

The bark of the Foambark contains a high concentration of saponin, a frothing compound, and was used by the Aborigines as a fish-poison. Most parts of the tree will produce foam if agitated in water. The umbrella-shaped crown is quite distinctive as is the ferny foliage which often flushes apricot-pink during growth spurts. When immature, the fruits are maroon, changing to yellowish-brown with age. Covered by fine penetrating hairs, fruits should be handled with care. The tree's natural range extends from Taree in New South Wales to the Bloomfield River south of Cooktown in north Queensland. It grows best on basaltic or alluvial soils.

**In the garden:** This small tree should be more widely cultivated as it is easy to grow if conditions are not too harsh. Full sun and mild frost are tolerated but ample water and soil nutrients make a dramatic difference to early growth and appearance. The seed capsules are ripe in spring and will open when dry to release the black seeds which sprout two weeks after sowing.

**Family:** *Sapindaceae*

39

*Kreysigia multiflora*

# Kreysigia

This lovely little plant with its wiry zig-zag stems, bright spear-shaped leaves and a flower at every leaf junction does not look like a member of the lily family. Suckers form around the base but do not spread extensively. In its habitat of rainforest and adjacent moist forests, the plant is often supported by other vegetation but under cultivation it develops a more compact shape. It is found growing naturally from the mid-north coast of New South Wales to south-east Queensland.

**In the garden:** It is hardy if given light shade and thick mulch. High soil fertility does not seem to be a major requirement. It makes a beautiful plant in a tub, whether or not it is flowering, and becomes a very bushy specimen. As an indoor plant it is reputed to look more attractive and flower more heavily than it does outside. Propagation is easiest by division.

**Family:** *Liliaceae*

*Leea indica*

# Bandicoot Berry

In tropical lowland rainforest, *Leea* sprawls alongside stream-banks and in other moist sheltered sites. Its foliage has an open arrangement with striking compound leaves up to 1m in length. Long-lasting fruits gradually darken from green through red-brown to black.

**In the garden:** Given a warm situation with protection from wind, *Leea* will quickly grow to 3m and will fruit while still young. Its vigorous habit is part of its attraction. For lightly-shaded positions it makes a beautiful foliage plant. Frost and cold conditions are not tolerated, especially when young, so that *Leea* is best grown in tropical or warm subtropical climates. The seed germinates readily.

**Family:** *Leeaceae*

Photo: Alex Hansa

*Lepidozamia peroffskyana*

# Burrawang Palm

This robust but very elegant cycad with its shiny evenly-arranged leaves, can grow to 5m but is more often seen under 2m. It occurs in moist open forest and rainforest margins from Taree in New South Wales north to Nambour in southern Queensland. It is well adapted to fire and sprouts a beautiful crown of new leaves if the old ones are damaged. The large cones are borne on female plants in summer and contain over one hundred orange seeds which are highly poisonous. The Aborigines were able to make use of the high starch content in the seed by roasting and soaking to remove the toxin.

**In the garden:** This slow-growing plant makes a superb specimen. It can be kept in a tub almost indefinitely and lasts well indoors. It needs protection from full sun and from frost although it is happy to grow in cold southern areas. Soil fertility does not need to be high but good drainage and moisture are important. Propagation is from seed which can take over twelve months to germinate. Mature specimens are difficult to transplant.

**Family:** *Zamiaceae*

41

*Lycopodium cernuum*

# Coral Fern

The name *Lycopodium* is formed from the Greek words *"lucos"* meaning wolf and *"podos"* meaning foot, and refers to the clawlike leaves. Wolf's Foot Fern is one of its alternative common names. In fact it is not a true fern – it belongs to the ancient family of Club Mosses, a dominant plant group 400 million years ago. Most Club Mosses are now small creeping plants but some of their early relatives were tree-sized. It is widespread in Queensland, New South Wales, Northern Territory and Western Australia as well as New Guinea, New Zealand and Polynesia. Whether growing under a rainforest canopy or in full sun it is a vigorous scrambler with erect stems reaching 1m.

**In the garden:** Coral Fern makes a pretty ground cover for moist or poorly drained soils in sun or shade. In a container it is very decorative and hardy, indoors or out. Once established it can look after itself but it is known for the difficulty with which it is transplanted. The creeping rhizome must be divided for successful propagation. The dried stems are used in flower arrangements.

**Family:** *Lycopodiaceae*

Photo: Alex Hansa

*Macadamia tetraphylla*

# Macadamia Nut

Rarely seen now in its natural state, this tree and its close relative *Macadamia integrifolia* are grown in extensive plantations for their delicious nuts. They are the only exclusively Australian plants so far grown commercially as a food crop. The stiff leaves are arranged in whorls of four (*"tetra"* means four and *"phylla"* means leaf), distinct from *M. integrifolia* with whorls of three leaves. This tree used to grow naturally from the Richmond River in New South Wales to the Numinbah and Coomera Rivers south of Brisbane.

**In the garden:** Macadamia Nut grows moderately fast into a bushy ornamental tree up to 10m in height. Its preference for deep rich soils with plenty of summer moisture should be followed as far as possible. However it will tolerate slightly less favourable conditions and produces nuts as far south as Sydney. Heavy mulching is most beneficial. Seeds germinate in two weeks and grow rapidly but seedlings may not bear fruit until several years after cutting–grown or grafted trees.

**Family:** *Proteaceae*

*Macaranga tanarius*

# Macaranga

Land-holders interested in land rehabilitation have a high opinion of this resourceful tree because of its ability to regenerate naturally on degraded rainforest land. The leaf is unusual, with the stalk attached almost in the centre of the large heart-shaped leaf blade. Flowers are greeny-yellow and the green fruits, on female trees only, are easily overlooked. It grows only in the warmer rainforest areas from the Richmond River in New South Wales to Cooktown in north Queensland and in south-east Asia.

**In the garden**: Macaranga is being grown increasingly as a foliage plant for containers, for general landscaping and for rainforest regeneration. It is very tough and will cope with full sun, wind and indifferent soil but is not tolerant of frost or even cold weather while less than 1m tall. Good soil conditions and plenty of water will give growth rates of over 2m per year. The round black seeds should be collected in autumn when the spiky capsules first open and sown immediately. The seedlings must be kept in a warm place throughout the first winter. It is easily struck from cuttings.

**Family:** *Euphorbiaceae*

Photo: Alex Hans.

*Mackinlaya macrosciadia*

# Mackinlaya

This symmetrical flowerhead will last for two months, gradually changing into a cluster of dark-fleshed blue-grey berries lasting for another few months. The leaves are reminiscent of the familiar Umbrella Tree, also in the family Araliaceae and also from Queensland. However, Mackinlaya is much smaller, sometimes multi-stemmed, and growing only from 2m to 3m in height and width and has an open sprawling habit. In coastal Queensland rainforests from Gympie to Cape York, it inhabits moist sheltered places along the banks of creeks.

**In the garden:** Mackinlaya is not widely grown but makes an interesting plant for shady places or indoors. Warm climates are preferred but it does well as far south as mid-coastal New South Wales if protected from frost and exposure. Seed can be collected in winter and germinates well, although slowly. Cuttings are also successful.

**Family:** *Araliaceae*

44

## *Mallotus discolor*
## Yellow Kamala

Yellow Kamala belongs to a family with over one thousand extremely varied species from all over the world, including tiny succulents and large cactus-like trees. This neat tree has a rounded crown and pretty fruits yielding a bright yellow dye. It grows in most rainforest areas, and in regrowth from the Clarence River in New South Wales north to Townsville in Queensland.

**In the garden:** Its compact shape at all ages makes it an admirable garden tree of 10m to 15m. Deep soil and plenty of summer moisture are preferred but it does well in less favourable sites, especially if given fertilizer. Cuttings are reasonably successful but seed, which can be collected in January, can be unpredictable even when sown fresh. If seed is more than two weeks old it is completely non-viable.

**Family:** *Euphorbiaceae*

## *Mallotus philippensis*
## Red Kamala

In India a golden-red dye for silk is made from the powder covering these fruits. Red Kamala is widespread through Asia and New Guinea and from north Queensland south to the Illawarra in New South Wales. It is a very common tree growing to about 10m and is most useful for regenerating abused ex-rainforest land, often unfortunately in competition with the introduced Camphor Laurel. Brilliant red and blue bugs often inhabit the foliage but do little harm to the tree.

**In the garden:** It is not a remarkably handsome tree and is rarely seen in cultivation. However it could be grown more often for reforestation purposes as it is very tough in full sun and in depleted soil. For a pioneer tree its seed is remarkably short-lived and it is difficult to find trees with good seed. It should be sown when very fresh.

**Family:** *Euphorbiaceae*

*Melia azedarach var. australasica*

# White Cedar

White Cedar is now so widely planted that it is often not recognized as originating in rainforest areas. Its lacy foliage is most noticeable in autumn when it turns bright yellow before falling. The perfumed flowers develop into fleshy fruits which are poisonous to humans, pigs and dogs but are liked by birds. Within Australia it occurs naturally from the Illawarra region in New South Wales to Cape York peninsula and also in Western Australia, but it can now be seen in many other inland and southern regions.

**In the garden:** Cultivated for many years for its beauty, speed and hardiness, it is easy to grow in many sites. Caterpillars often defoliate the tree in autumn but this can be coped with by encircling the trunk with a broad collar of cellotape, sticky side out. Alternatively the collar can be light metal with an overhanging flange at the top; the caterpillars climb the trunk, collect under the flange and can be destroyed each morning. Seed can be gathered in winter and germinates well without any treatment.

**Family:** *Meliaceae*

*Metrosideros queenslandicus*

# Queensland Golden Myrtle

Spectacular golden flowers, dense foliage and coppery-red new growth have made this one of the most beautiful of the rainforest plants yet it is so far little known in cultivation. Within its very restricted range at high altitudes on the Atherton Tableland in north Queensland, it grows as a 30m tree, usually on granite or metamorphic soils with a moderately high rainfall supplemented by mists in the dry time of the year.

**In the garden:** In the open this plant reaches only 8m and as a garden shrub is more often 3m to 4m. The foliage is rarely without its bright tips even in winter. Full sun is required for best flowering as even the shady side of the plant will flower less well. Good drainage, plenty of moisture in the early stages and applications of fertilizer are important otherwise it will grow slowly. At least as far south as Sydney it can be grown easily and once established will tolerate moderate frosts. Cuttings strike easily and the fine seed can be germinated in fibrous peaty material.

**Family:** *Myrtaceae*

Photo: Alex Hansa

*Millettia megasperma*

# Native Wistaria

This is one of the very heavy woody vines seen in subtropical rainforest where often the only sign of it is a carpet of purple flowers on the ground or the large furry pods with their bulky seeds. The flowers are as prolific as the introduced Wistaria but the leaves are retained all year round. Its natural range extends only from the Richmond River in northern New South Wales to Fraser Island.

**In the garden:** Generally this climber prefers warm latitudes with good soil and moisture. However it does grow on sand at Fraser Island and can cope with cold once established. By natural inclination it forms a canopy over surrounding vegetation and needs plenty of scope with strong supports. If space is available it makes a very showy, fast-growing and reliable climber. Seed can be collected in winter, germinates easily without treatment and grows quickly.

**Family:** *Fabaceae*

47

## *Nauclea orientalis*
## Leichhardt Tree

Golfball-sized flowers are partly hidden under the new spring foliage of *Nauclea*. It is a magnificent 15m to 20m tree growing in tropical coastal areas of Queensland, New Guinea and Indonesia in swampy or moist areas of rainforest or along streams in open forest. *Nauclea* was used extensively by coastal Aborigines for many purposes. The trunk was used to make canoes, the leaves and bark were made into fish poisons, medicines and pain-killers and the bitter fruit was eaten (from "Mutooroo" see Bibliography). The bark yields a bright yellow dye, explaining one of its common names, Canary Wood.

**In the garden:** Generally this tree is too large for most gardens but it is outstandingly beautiful, with a liking for poorly drained soils – an unusual combination. Although a tropical plant, it copes surprisingly well with light frost. Both in cultivation and in natural conditions it is a good host for epiphytic plants. Seed from the boat-shaped fruit germinates readily.

**Family:** *Naucleaceae*

Photo: Alex Hansa

## *Omalanthus populifolius*
## Bleeding Heart

This beautiful pioneer tree is adept at rapidly filling gaps in rainforest or recolonizing cleared land. In Sydney it has become a very common regeneration species. Young trees have huge heart-shaped leaves up to 30cm across, three times the size of the leaves on older trees. A few bright red dying leaves are always present and in summer brown pigeons flock to eat the dull purple fruits. Its extensive distribution, from the far south of New South Wales to Cape York peninsula and beyond to New Guinea and Indonesia, demonstrates its adaptability.

**In the garden:** Grown in sun or shade, this is a particularly successful specimen. Although only a shrub or small tree up to 5m, it can grow 3m in the first year with optimum moisture, soil drainage and nutrient levels. Frost will burn the tips of a small plant but it will recover in spring. It makes a splendid tub plant although it quickly outgrows its container if not pruned regularly. Propagation is very easy from cuttings or from seed which is ready in late summer and must be sown fresh.

**Family:** *Euphorbiaceae*

*Oreocallis pinnata*

## Dorrigo Waratah

Two Greek words give Oreocallis its name – *"oreos"* meaning mountain, referring to its habitat, and *"calos"* meaning beautiful and referring to the flowers. These are very striking and attract numerous birds and insects in spring and summer. The light green leaves are also attractive, especially on young trees. In its highland habitat the tree can grow over 20m tall and, while it was still plentiful, was sought after as an ornamental cabinet wood. The only places where it can be found naturally are the Dorrigo Plateau in New South Wales and the ranges on the Queensland-New South Wales border.

**In the garden:** In cultivation Dorrigo Waratah flowers when only a few metres tall and rarely tops 10m. For such a desirable tree it is both difficult to obtain and to cultivate. Although growing naturally on poorer soils in cool conditions, young plants seem to resent anything less than excellent soil, perfect drainage and good protection from both frost and sun. Once established to 2m it will survive. Seed, ripe between February and June is hard to find but germinates quite well. Cuttings will strike, though not with ease.

**Family:** *Proteaceae*

*Oreocallis* sp.

# Tree Waratah

This tree has commonly but mistakenly been called *Oreocallis wickhamii*. Known for its beautiful pink timber, it is also regarded as one of the most striking of the rainforest trees. Once seen as a large tree, it has largely disappeared along with it natural habitat on the Atherton Tableland as a result of clearing for agriculture.

**In the garden:** Grown outside tall rainforest, this tree reaches only 10m and develops a busny crown of dark leaves. It flowers most profusely when grown in full sun in deep rich soil with extra water during hot dry periods. As a highland tree it adapts well to cool climates and flowers in Melbourne. Seed germination is rapid but subsequent growth can be slow unt the adult leaves appear at 2 to 3 years and flowering may not occur for 8 to 10 years. Cutting-grown plants flower within one year at 1m high. A tendency when very young towards chlorosis, or yellowing of the leaves, can be overcome with applications of iron chelates to the soil, together with added nitrogen.

**Family:** *Proteaceae*

*Orites excelsa*

## Mountain Silky Oak

Saddle-frames, wine casks and shingles were some of the articles made from this highly ornamental tree last century. Mountain Silky Oak can be tall but is often seen as a bushy shrub, the foliage and flowers being very dense in open situations. Its genus name *"Orites"* mean mountaineer – it occurs at high altitudes in rainforests from the Hunter River in New South Wales to Mt. Mistake south-west of Brisbane and again in north Queensland.

**In the garden:** It is an admirable garden plant that is not very fussy about soil fertility as long as moisture is available. Full sun is acceptable only if not accompanied by exposure to wind. The lobed juvenile leaves make it a beautiful tub-plant which does well indoors. Seed, ripe in autumn, is easy to germinate but difficult to collect as it tends to be shed very suddenly.

**Family:** *Proteaceae*

*Orthosiphon aristatus*

## Cat's Moustache

Four long stamens, about twice as long as the rest of the flower form the whiskers of Cat's Moustache, also called Cat's Whiskers. The summer flowers can occur in shades of pale pink and lavender as well as white. A lover of moist places, in sun or shade this softwood perennial reaches a height of 1m with a similar spread. It occurs naturally on the tropical coast of Queensland from Cardwell north and also in south-east Asia.

**In the garden:** A fast-growing plant, it has long been known in cultivation in tropical and subtropical areas for the ease with which it can be grown. Regular pruning is necessary to keep it relatively tidy although new plants can be so easily propagated from cutting that it may not be worth maintaining old plants. It is frost tender and not suitable for cold districts except under cover.

**Family:** *Lamiaceae*

Photo: Alex Hansa

*Pandorea jasminoides*

# Bower of Beauty

In full sun, high on top of the forest canopy, this climber flowers unseen from below. Its popularity in cultivation is well justified because of its beautiful dark glossy foliage and the flowers which bloom for months. They vary from pink with a crimson throat to a pure white form. Its natural habitat is coastal rainforest in the subtropical areas of northern New South Wales and south-east Queensland.

**In the garden:** This is possibly the best rainforest creeper for gardens. It is remarkably hardy, grown as a climber or a ground cover and is happy in full sun and wind as long as its roots are cool and moist with reasonable soil nutrients. It does well as far south as Melbourne if given some protection from frost. Although naturally a large creeper, regular pruning can induce a compact habit. Cuttings strike readily.

**Family:** *Bignoniaceae*

*Pararchidendron pruinosum*
(formerly *Abarema sapindoides* )

# Snow Wood

This lovely little tree is sometimes given the unflattering name of Stinkwood due to the strong but not unpleasant smell given off when it is cut. Far more noticeable are the pom-pom flowers in spring which change from white to deep yellow with age. The orange seed pods which follow are tightly twisted with shiny hard black seeds inside. Often seen growing on rainforest edges where it forms a dense bank of foliage, it occurs naturally from the Illawarra region in New South Wales to the Atherton Tableland in north Queensland.

**In the garden:** Its graceful appearance and light green lacy leaves make it an excellent 5m to 8m plant for shrubberies. Although tolerant of cool conditions and able to grow in southern Australia, it is sensitive to heavy frost. When protected from wind, it is hardy in full sun and will develop very thick foliage. Specimens can be kept in tubs for some time and used indoors for short periods.

**Family:** *Mimosaceae*

*Pittosporum rhombifolium*

# Hollywood

Queensland Pittosporum, Diamond-leaved Pittosporum and White Holly are all commonly used alternative names for this small tree. It is usually noticed when the whole crown turns white with flowers then orange with massed fruits lasting for three months over autumn. Leaves are glossy and diamond-shaped, forming a neat tree, often pyramidal in outline when grown in the open. Frequently seen in rainforest regrowth, it occurs on rich soils from the Richmond River in New South Wales to Forty Mile Scrub, west of Cairns in Queensland.

**In the garden:** It is successful in cultivation, particularly as a street tree, because it is so hardy and reliable. Rich soil and plenty of water speed up early growth, which can be slow, and will ensure a dense silhouette. Light frost does not seem to be a problem. Fruits collected ripe should be dried to split the orange case and the black seed planted without delay. Germination may take two to three months.

**Family:** *Pittosporaceae*

Hollywood in flower
(description above)

53

*Pittosporum undulatum*

# Sweet Pittosporum

This beautiful plant perfumes the surrounding area with its white flowers in spring. For that reason it is sometimes called Native Daphne although not related to the exotic Daphne. The long-lasting fruits contain sticky seeds that adhere to birds' bills and become widely dispersed. Its natural distribution was broad even before it became an established horticultural plant. It occurs in South Australia, Tasmania, Victoria, New South Wales and south-eastern Queensland in a variety of rainforest and moist open country habitats.

**In the garden:** Great adaptability and rapid growth make this an excellent low windbreak or screen plant reaching 8m to 10m. Fertile soil and plenty of water will produce faster growth and handsome foliage, but less favourable conditions will not greatly affect the quality of its appearance. Cuttings strike well and seed is produced in great quantities in autumn, germinating readily. The sticky seeds can be separated by rubbing in sand prior to sowing.

**Family:** *Pittosporaceae*

54

*Podocarpus elatus*

# Plum Pine

Although the swollen stalks of the fruit are sweetish and quite edible, they are hardly as delectable as a plum. They are dropped in multitudes below the female trees in autumn. The narrow leaves are very noticeable when they first shoot, with colours ranging from pinkish red to shiny pale green. Uncommon now as a tall tree, Plum Pine is recorded in the warmer rainforests, particularly those close to the coast from the Illawarra region in New South Wales to Cairns.

**In the garden:** For some years it remains as a dense shrub, eventually becoming a shade tree from 10m to 20m in height. Growth in the early stages is slow but Plum Pine can be kept as a handsome tub plant until 2m high before planting out. High moisture and nutrition levels will encourage darker leaves and a faster growth rate. Cutting-grown plants, from trees selected for their attractive shape, are often used if uniformity is required. Seed germinates in four weeks.

**Family:** *Podocarpaceae*

*Polyscias elegans*

# Celerywood

When cut, the bark of this tree both tastes and smells of celery, hence the common name. As the scientific species name suggests, it is an elegant tree with long leaves divided into small shiny leaflets bunched at the ends of the branches, rather like a palm. The mature seeds attract flocks of currawongs and fig birds in autumn and winter, ensuring its spread as a hardy pioneer tree. Commonly seen in rainforest regrowth on volcanic soil, it grows from the Illawarra region in New South Wales to Thursday Island, north of Cape York.

**In the garden:** Fast-growing but not dominating, Celerywood rarely exceeds 15m and is happy in sun or shade. It has a preference for plenty of water, fertile soil and warm conditions. However it will settle for a lot less and still look fine. Tub plants are especially attractive. Propagation can be difficult as many trees bear infertile seed.

**Family:** *Araliaceae*

*Quintinia verdonii*

## Grey Possumwood

This is an example of a limited number of tree species whose fine seeds germinate in the moist fibrous trunks of tree ferns. Rose-leaf Marara (*Caldcluvia paniculosa*), Callicoma (*Callicoma serratifolia*) and Brown Possumwood (*Quintinia sieberi*) are all able to start life similarly above the ground, before gradually sending down roots to establish in the soil. Possumwood becomes a spreading tree of 10m to 15m, usually growing in cool sites either at high altitudes or along creek banks where temperatures are lower than in the surrounding forest. It occurs from the mid-north coast of New South Wales to the Blackall Range near Nambour in Queensland.

**In the garden:** Moderately fast-growing in the early stages, Possumwood makes a handsome plant with its red-tipped leaves and profuse flowers. Its preference for cool places enables it to adapt to temperate climates if protected from frost. Soil fertility does not need to be high, but help from fertilizers and plenty of water will promote bright leaf colour. It strikes from cuttings and can be grown from seed, ready in mid-summer. The seed must be collected before the capsules open.

**Family:** *Escalloniaceae*

*Rhododendron lochae*

# Native Rhododendron

Australia's only native rhododendron is restricted to altitudes over 1000m on some of the highest peaks in north Queensland. It grows in exposed positions and is accustomed to rainfall of 4000mm (160″) per year, frequently augmented by drenching mountain mists. In natural conditions it develops as a spreading shrub up to 5m in height but under cultivation it is considerably smaller and more compact, often less than 1m high and wide. The flowers are very striking when they bloom in spring and summer.

**In the garden:** Rhododendron can be enjoyed in shady east coast and southern gardens provided it is kept well watered and is grown in a very well-drained soil medium such as orchid mix or fibrous compost. It is not suitable for hot dry regions. When grown in a tub its preferred conditions can be provided and the plant can be brought inside when in flower. Propagation from cuttings and seed is successful.

**Family:** *Ericaceae*

Photo: Alex Hansa

*Schizomeria ovata*

# Crabapple

Crabapple is sometimes called Snowberry for its white, juicy fruits. These are edible and are an important food source for rainforest pigeons. Tall and narrow in forest situations, it is a spreading tree from 10m to 15m in height when growing in the open. It often occurs with Coachwood (*Ceratopetalum apetalum*) on poorer soils, often in the process of recolonizing marginal eucalypt forest with rainforest species. In range it extends from southern New South Wales to Fraser Island in Queensland.

**In the garden:** Crabapple is little known in cultivation, but is well worth growing for its dense foliage and the beautiful young leaves sprouting in varying shades of pink and pale green. Growth is fastest if shelter is provided for the first two years as well as regular water and fertilizer. Germination of seeds is both erratic and extremely slow.

**Family:** *Cunoniaceae*

*Scolopia braunii*

# Flintwood

Rainforest trees of little use to the first white settlers were often identified by the problems they caused in being chopped down, for instance Steelwood (*Sarcopteryx stipitata*) Iron-wood (*Rhodamnia acuminata*) Axe-breaker (*Geijera paniculata*) and this tree, Flintwood. Although recorded up to 25m in the original forests, it is almost always much smaller and in open situations may be only 5m to 8m with a very compact shape. Several times each year young leaves flush a beautiful dark red and on juvenile trees they are diamond-shaped. Small creamy-white flowers appear in spring, and in summer and autumn the berries change from yellow through red to black. It grows from the Illawarra region in New South Wales to Cape York peninsula.

**In the garden:** Flintwood is a very ornamental small tree for sun or shade. It is not a fast grower, making it a long-lasting tub-plant. If kept growing actively with ample water and fertilizer it will produce colourful new leaves throughout the year. Much of the copious fruit produced does not contain seed; cuttings could be more worthwhile.

**Family:** *Flacourtiaceae*

## Sloanea australis
# Maiden's Blush

This tree was named by timber-workers for the colour of its heartwood. It is mostly noticed for its vigorous coppicing habit, the main trunk often being almost hidden by the new stems. The young toothed leaves are a beautiful pink, another possible reason for the name. These spring flowers develop into decorative woody capsules containing three or four black seeds, covered in an orange aril and eagerly sought after by birds. The capsules are used in flower arrangements. Maiden's Blush loves water and can grow into a large buttressed tree near creeks in coastal rainforests from Bateman's Bay in New South Wales to north Queensland.

**In the garden:** Rarely over 15m outside a forest situation, this tree prefers shady sheltered locations and will not tolerate drying out. Grown in a tub it will live for years as an attractive bush, provided its tips are pinched out to encourage branching. Cuttings and even woody branches send out roots readily. Seed, collected in late summer, germinates in a few weeks.

**Family:** *Elaeocarpaceae*

## Stenocarpus salignus
# Scrub Beefwood

An alternative common name, Red Silky Oak, also refers to the dark red colour of the timber. Rainforest trees are often classified in Australia as "softwoods", differentiated from the eucalypt "hardwoods". However, many rainforest trees have very hard wood, as does this one, and they can be grouped with the hardwoods as distinct from the pines which are the real softwoods. The tree is variable in appearance and height from a 30m sparsely-crowned forest tree to a 10m tree with a dense rounded crown. From the mid-south coast of New South Wales to Rockhampton in Queensland, it grows usually at high altitudes, although in the south of its range it occurs down to sea level.

**In the garden:** The summer flowers form dense clusters and can appear when the tree is very young, which is fortunate as it is quite slow-growing. In natural conditions Scrub Beefwood is adapted to poor, often stony soils, but to look attractive as an ornamental tree it needs rich well-drained soil. In autumn the narrow fruits release flat, easily germinated seeds.

**Family:** *Proteaceae*

*Stenocarpus sinuatus*

# Firewheel Tree
or Wheel of Fire

The flowers of this well-known tree bloom inside the outer foliage giving it a spectacular glowing appearance. A dense columnar silhouette and very dark glossy leaves distinguish the tree from its close relatives in the Proteaceae family. Most types of rainforest from the Nambucca River near Coff's Harbour in New South Wales to the Atherton Tableland in Queensland will contain Firewheel trees.

**In the garden:** Although a tall timber tree in the forest, it rarely tops 15m in cultivation. Plenty of water in summer and applications of fertilizer will produce quite rapid growth contrary to its unfortunate reputation. Protection from frost and wind exposure is worthwhile in the early stages below 2m. Grown in a container, it is very striking and can be used indoors. Seed can be collected in summer, just as the first capsules open, and germinates within three weeks.

**Family:** *Proteaceae*

*Syzygium cormiflorum*

# White Apple

Flowers and fruit sprout on the main trunk from ground level on this remarkable north Queensland Lilly-Pilly. It occurs from Townsville to Iron Range on Cape York peninsula in two forms. The ramiflorous form, flowering on the branches like *S.moorei* (p. 62) is a large tree usually found in lowland areas. The cauliflorous form pictured here flowers on the trunk and is a smaller tree, more common in the highlands. The profuse flowers open in winter and are highly popular with lorikeets but the large white fruits are not used greatly by wildlife.

**In the garden:** Both forms develop into a tree of about 10m in the open that can be grown easily if given ample summer water and reasonably well-drained soil. The cauliflorous form is more suited for southern areas. Shelter from frost is important for young plants. Like all the Lilly-Pillies, White Apple makes a handsome tub plant when young. Seeds germinate quickly if they are fresh.

**Family:** *Myrtaceae*

*ygium hodgkinsoniae*

## d Lilly-Pilly

Due to widespread destruction of subtropical riverine rainforest, this plant is now rare and endangered in its natural tat between the Richmond River in New South Wales and Gympie in Queensland. These large honey-scented flowers be very profuse when they bloom in winter and the robust fruit is an eye-catching red. The foliage of this compact shrub glossy rich green.

ne garden: It is a very handsome shrub, growing to 4m if given some shelter and a fairly rich soil. When very young the t goes through a stage of almost zero growth coupled with a peculiar bunching of the new shoots. It is worth htaining the plant in a tub for two years until this stage is passed. Full sun will slow growth markedly but light frost does seem to be a great problem. Seed can be collected at varying times, germinating easily and often as multiple shoots.

ily: *Myrtaceae*

61

*Syzygium luehmannii*

# Riberry
or Small-leaved Lilly-Pilly

Riberry is an outstandingly beautiful plant either as a 30m forest tree or as a 5m to 10m shrub in cultivation. Its trunk produces millable logs but it is far more widely known now as one the best Lilly-Pillies in horticulture. From Kempsey in New South Wales to Cooktown in Queensland, it grows in most of the warmer rainforests on sand or deep rich soil and from high altitudes to within 20m of the beach.

**In the garden:** The dense weeping foliage flows right to the ground and new growth changes through a range of bright to pastel pinks for several weeks at least twice a year. It is hardy anywhere on the east of Australia, except in very cold or very dry areas, and can be grown in full sun or partial shade. Fertile soils with good water supply produce the best leaf displays. It makes a superb tub plant that can be brought inside for short periods while the leaves are at their brightest. Propagation from seed is easy and germination occurs in 3 to 4 weeks. Cuttings are also successful.

**Family:** *Myrtaceae*

*Syzygium moorei*

# Rose Apple
or Coolamon

Early settlers called this the Watermelon tree for the colour of the flowers, borne completely inside the crown on every available branch. The large white fruit formed in autumn is juicy and edible, though insipid in flavour. Rose Apple is one of the most impressive of the tall rainforest trees, with its thick trunk and dense crown of large glossy leaves. It is included in the rare and endangered plant list, being restricted to a few sites in lowland subtropical rainforest from the Richmond, Brunswick and Tweed River valleys north to Tallebudgera, south of Brisbane.

**In the garden:** Well-drained humus-rich soil, plenty of water and help from fertilizers will give steady growth. Scale insects can cause a sooty mould on the leaves, and psillids, a kind of sucking insect, can cause leaf-dimpling in young plants. However these problems either do not occur in mature trees or are not noticed. Germination can take several months but is quite successful, as are healthy tip-cuttings.

**Family:** *Myrtaceae*

*ygium wilsonii* ssp. *wilsonii*

# wderpuff Lilly-Pilly

While slender and straggling as an understorey shrub in dense tropical rainforest. Powderpuff Lilly-Pilly in cultivation is
of the most attractive and colourful of the rainforest shrubs. The branches and foliage are weeping in habit with frequent
hes of bright reddish-brown new leaves. White clusters of fruits follow the crimson flowers. It occurs in Queensland's
stal rainforests from Ingham to Cooktown usually below 700m in altitude and on relatively poor soils.

**he garden:** For a lowland tropical species it grows and flowers remarkably well as far south as Sydney. Regular use of
lizer and water will promote plenty of new leaf growth and heavy flowering. Although reputed to dislike full sun and
, it can cope with both if not too severe. However it looks best in a warm position with partial shade where it will grow
spreading 2m to 3m shrub. Scale and sooty mould can be a problem. Propagated from cuttings or fresh seed, it grows
ly but steadily.

**ily:** *Myrtaceae*

64

Red Cedar (description oppos

*Toona australis*

# Red Cedar

Renowned for its wonderful timber and the speed with which it disappeared after the coming of Europeans, it is not so well-known as a fast-growing and handsome shade tree. In winter, its leaves turn yellow and drop but within weeks the new pink shoots appear. Formerly widespread from the Illawarra region in New South Wales to the McIlwraith Range on the north-east of Cape York peninsula it grew mostly in moist rainforests on fertile soils. It also occurs in New Guinea.

**In the garden:** Red Cedar needs plenty of room and may reach 20m in height in the open. It is easily grown in full sun if given adequate moisture, fertilizer and protection from heavy frost in the first two years. Large numbers are now being replanted privately for reforestation although they are unlikely to develop straight trunks due to the branching effect of tip-moth damage. Seed can be gathered in December or January as the capsules begin to open and germinates within two or three weeks.

**Family:** *Meliaceae*

*Tristaniopsis laurina*
(formerly *Tristania laurina*)

# Water Gum

Water Gums favour stream-bank locations and some magnificently gnarled old specimens, veterans of many floods, can be found near creeks in and around rainforest from Gippsland in Victoria to Gympie in Queensland. The young leaves are usually maroon and in cold weather the whole tree may redden. Old trees in favourable sites can grow to 20m but it is most often found as a shrub or tree between 5m and 10m.

**In the garden:** This handsome tree deserves to be grown more often as a rapid screen plant and an excellent fill-in for eucalypt windbreaks. It copes with cold, medium frost, wet soil, low fertility and full sun. However, good conditions and regular fertilizer will produce a more attractive tree. It germinates rather slowly from seed which can be collected in autumn before the capsules open.

**Family:** *Myrtaceae*

*Triunia youngiana*

# Spice Bush

The enormously varied Proteaceae family was named after the Greek god "Proteus" who was capable of changing his form at will. The family includes the Macadamias with their delicious nuts and Spice Bush which bears these highly poisonous fruits. As a rule very few fruits are set – this bunch was exceptional. The flowers are far more numerous and are very beautiful white or pale lilac. A delicious honeysuckle scent surrounds the plant when flowering just before Christmas. New leaves shoot as a beautiful coppery pink covered in silver hairs. It is rarely seen over 2m and grows in low light as an understorey plant. Favoured habitat is the cooler mountain rainforests between Dorrigo in New South Wales and south-east Queensland.

**In the garden:** This very attractive shrub will grow in light to heavy shade. Good soil and ample moisture are needed to produce plenty of colourful new growth. Tub plants need to be nipped back to discourage a slightly straggling habit. Seed collected in winter, is scarce and germinates slowly.

**Family:** *Proteaceae*

66

*Trochocarpa laurina*

# Tree Heath

This small tree is the only one in the Australian heath family to reach tree size. Its coloured leaves with their distinctive parallel veins change through brilliant reds and pinks, when they first shoot, to the more pastel colours seen here. As a shrub or small tree of 5m to 6m, it is seen on poorer soils in rainforest or adjoining eucalypt forest from southern NSW to southern Queensland and on two peaks in far north Queensland. The small white flowers occur in almost any month, likewise the navy-blue fruits, making it a useful and reliable food tree for bower-birds and other fruit-eaters.

**In the garden:** Attractive foliage, colourful for much of the year, and always densely arranged, is the feature for which this tree is grown either in the ground or as a beautiful container plant. Hardy in full sun or part shade, it tolerates cool conditions and poor soil though fertilizer will improve its appearance. High moisture levels are preferred, particularly in summer. In propagation, both cuttings and seeds are slow to form roots, seeds taking up to two years.

**Family:** *Epacridaceae*

*Viola hederacea*

# Native Violet

This little scentless violet is almost as familiar now in cultivation as the Sweet Violet. Lush green and rarely without flowers, it spreads wherever shelter and moisture are available. It has an enormous natural range along the east coast of Australia, including Tasmania and South Australia and is not confined to rainforest.

**In the garden:** It adapts with ease to many different soil types if some shade and moderate water are provided. Successful recovery is made even after severe stress such as frostbite or drying-out. In hanging baskets, festoons of flowering plantlets droop 1m or more. Extra plants can easily be obtained by separating young rooted plantlets.

**Family:** *Violaceae*

# Gardening with Rainforest Plants

Rainforest species display a staggering diversity of shape, colour, size and appearance. Their attraction is due not only to their flowers, spectacular as some of these are, but to the plant forms, leaf shapes, colourful new growth or bright fruits which are often just as interesting. Unlike plants from the drier parts of Australia, the seeds of most rainforest plants are distributed by birds or fruit bats rather than by the wind. Accordingly, the fruits look attractive and often develop brilliant colours and juicy or sweet flesh. The new leaves can be very striking and even more impressive than the flowers.

In gardens, plants can look radically different from their forest-grown counterparts. Shrubs or trees often grow tall, slender or straggling under a heavy forest canopy, where restricted root-space and light-space force growth upward. In the open, they will develop a shorter, denser and more rounded appearance. As a general rule, a tree grown in the open will be one-third the size of the same species in the rainforest.

Rainforest plants are remarkably hardy and adaptable. It is true that rainforest ecosystems are extremely finely balanced and can be damaged or destroyed by heavy-handed or prolonged interference. However, no gardener is attempting to set up a complete ecosystem in his or her back garden. We do not attempt to create a perfect ecological niche for an avocado or allamanda or any other foreign rainforest plant. Rather we provide conditions the plant will accept and which will make it behave as we would like, that is, flowering and fruiting more heavily, or growing more densely.

Natural growing conditions for different species can vary greatly, ranging from exposure to sun and salt winds on coastal headlands to perpetually wet and cool mountain gullies, from pure sand to poorly drained and claggy soils. In addition, some species are specifically adapted to recolonizing disturbed areas after natural catastrophes, whether isolated tree-falls or fire or cyclones. These plants, called pioneers, are usually fast-growing, tough, able to withstand full sun or wind, and often frost as well. Most of the so-called climax species which develop in the initial shelter of the pioneer trees, and which are considered to be sensitive, are in fact well-adapted to full sun on their crowns, lowered humidity and a broad range of temperatures.

Some rainforest plants grow very rapidly, particularly the pioneer species, which can grow 3m or more each year. Other species grow only moderately quickly and still others are quite slow. An impression of rainforest plants as slow growers may have arisen from the ability of many of them to wait indefinitely for a space to grow into. A closed canopy restricts active growth so severely that a small tree of 2m to 3m may be many years old. When a large tree falls, making a rift in the canopy, formerly dormant saplings grow quickly in the improved light. The first sapling there fills the space, consigning the others to more years of waiting. In garden conditions, a tree will develop faster but to a lesser height than it would in the forest.

Many of the most successful garden plants came from tropical, subtropical or temperate rainforest in other countries. Selected for the best forms, grown in open garden conditions and given fertilizer and water, they are deservedly popular. Australian rainforest plants are often more appealing in the garden than many of the exotic species but they are little known as yet. In addition they are often better suited to the relatively moist east coast gardens

than the drier native plants which have been planted indiscriminately and expected to do well simply because they are native.

Australian rainforest plants are being increasingly grown in gardens for their ability to attract birds. Lorikee[?] rosellas, honey-eaters, bower birds, native pigeons, currawongs and many others are enticed by the flowers[?] fruits.

Neither a large garden nor years of gardening expert[?] are required to grow rainforest plants at home. Australia[?] rainforest plants can be grown in most east coast garden[?] provided they are protected from extremes of heat, cold and exposure. Depending on the space available, they ca[?] be used to underplant an existing garden with extra species, or to form shrubberies either on their own or in combination with other natives or exotics. They can also used as specimen shrubs or trees in prominent position[?] as small rainforest communities with trees, shrubs, grou[?] covers, vines and ferns. Most of the shrubs and trees are very long-lived and will not need to be replaced. Even th[?] so-called "short-lived" pioneers will last at least twenty years.

Rainforest plants are becoming more readily availabl[?] from native plant nurseries. It may be necessary to ask sm[?] local nurseries to order them.

## Planning

Species should be selected that are suitable for the latitude, altitude, soil type and degree of exposure. If possible, planting sites should be chosen which are sheltered at least to some extent by buildings, existing tr[?] or fences. Most rainforest plants will tolerate strong sunl[?] if dessicating winds are minimized and frost damage lessened by the proximity of other trees. In new or spars[?] planted gardens, there is little choice, so hardy sun-lovin[?] plants should be used. Rapid cover can be provided by a[?] of the pioneer plants such as Brown Kurrajong, Pink As[?] Macaranga or Bleeding Heart. Well-drained soil is prefe[?] though there are various species which can tolerate poo[?] drainage.

Spacing depends entirely on the desired shape of the plants. If grown singly, most rainforest trees and shrubs will form a very rounded, bushy outline. Group planting can be spaced at roughly 2m intervals to allow some roo[?] for development but many gardeners will prefer closer planting to give quick cover.

## Mulching

Heavy mulching is important in keeping the root zo[?] cool, which is of more concern to these plants than overhead shade. Within two or three years, the combination of mulching and dense foliage can almost completely eliminate weeds. All garden refuse, lawn clippings, leaves and even branches can be used to buil[?] up humus. Once a canopy is established, conditions at ground level will remain moist, helping to break down [?] organic matter rapidly. If mulch cannot be provided in t[?] first few years, competition from weeds and grass must kept down by other means such as the use of low-toxic[?] herbicides. Although such sprays are undesirable, grass competition is equally unnatural from the plant's point [?] view and far more damaging.

## atering

Water is the most important factor in keeping rainforest
nts healthy, although this may not in fact necessitate
e water than is received by the average garden of
ventional exotics. Crucial times for water needs are the
three months after planting and during hot, dry, windy
mers such as Melbourne often experiences. A good
< once or twice a week during dry spells may be
essary for young plants, but established ones are
arkably resistant, especially if mulched well.

## rtilizing

Clearly, deep rich soil is the ideal. However, most
deners work with something less. In rainforests, soil
rients are recycled rapidly as fallen leaves decompose
are again made available to the roots. To hasten the
blishment of this natural cycle, fertilizers can be used in
early years, helping the plants to grow quickly and
in producing leaf litter for their own use. Compost or
manure are excellent natural fertilizers but if these are
readily available then a handful of slow release
mical fertilizer twice a year, or a high nitrogen quick-
ase fertilizer three or four times during spring, summer
autumn, will give encouraging results. All artificial
lizers should be well watered in and covered with
ch. Lime should be applied with caution as acid soils
normal for rainforest plants.

## uning

These plants respond well to pruning, usually
eloping a very bushy crown of new growth. Pruning
be carried out at any time of the year but the bare
earance will be soonest covered if it is done in late
mer. Water and fertilizer should be provided to
ourage fresh new growth. Pinching out the tips of
ng plants to encourage low branching is preferable to
ge pruning later.

## opagation

Growing new plants is easy for those with the time and
est to be assiduous in their care. Many plants will
e from cuttings, using healthy new growth. They are
grown under cover, preferably with automatic misting
bottom heat. Various simple methods are detailed in
e Encyclopaedia of Australian Plants" and in
stralian Native Plants". (See Bibliography)
n seedling propagation, fresh seed is essential.
ection from the parent tree itself is best as seed
ered from the ground is often already damaged by
cts or has lost its viability. All seed should be examined
ully and one or two of them cut in half to determine
state of health, healthy kernels being firm and white
een. Nearly all seeds, except for the very fine ones,
ld be soaked for 24 hours prior to planting. Pure sand
es an excellent medium as it minimizes risk of
ping-off from fungus, but it does need careful watering.
lings can be potted up into a well-drained mix made
f fifty percent sand or gravel and fifty percent peat, old
ust or compost and kept under light shade until the
are established.

# Growing rainforest plants in tubs

Most rainforest plants make handsome container plants.
Their unusual foliage and bright growth tips are their main
attraction but some species, particularly when grown from
cuttings, will produce flowers and fruits. Many of them can
also be used as indoor plants, varying only in the length of
time they continue to look attractive. That may range from
two weeks to several years. If grown in portable tubs, they
can be kept outside and moved inside when in flower or
new leaf.

In natural conditions, water and soil nutrients are
usually available at the higher soil levels so a deep
penetrating tap root is not required and in fact often dies
after a few years, being replaced by a mass of lateral roots.
If root-space is restricted the plant simply slows down its
growth. For these reasons, healthy container-grown
rainforest plants can last for some years, growing quite
slowly, and can then be planted out without the problems
of a curled tap root.

These plants can be grown as single specimens, or
planted closely in groups. If the container is large, a mixed
planting gives an interesting and original effect. When
grown for use on patios or verandahs they will look
splendid in bright light with some protection from wind
and hot sun. However, species can be chosen which will
cope with a perpetually shady south-wall position or with
full sun on the northern side.

Cultivation requirements for tubbed plants are similar
to those for garden-grown plants, with the exception of the
soil mix. A plant growing well in garden soil will not thrive
if that same soil is used in a tub, as it will almost certainly
cease to drain adequately. The potting medium must
contain at least one-third sand or aggregate and the rest
should be highly fibrous water-holding material, such as
good quality compost, with a small amount of soil.
Frequent light pruning, coupled with the use of slow-
release fertilizer, will produce shapely plants with dense
foliage. Water needs obviously depend on the soil mix, the
season, the plant and the position. However it is best to err
on the side of under-watering because wilting due to
dryness can be easily rectified whilst wilting from root
fungus attack cannot. Rainforest plants are in fact very
resistant to soil fungi but consistent over-watering causes
root problems.

Repotting should not be undertaken too frequently nor
into too large a container as this can induce very rapid,
leggy growth. Occasionally it can cause the death of the
plant if large amounts of fertilizer become available to a
very small root mass.

# Bibliography

Cribb, A.B. & J.W., **Wild Food in Australia,** Collins, 1974.

Elliott, W.R. & Jones, D.L., **Encyclopaedia of Australian Plants, Vols. 1,2,3.** Lothian 1981, 1982 & 1984.

Fairhill Native Plants, **Australian Native Plants for Subtropical & Tropical East Coast Gardens.**

Floyd, A.G., **Rainforest Trees of Mainland South-eastern Australia,** Forestry Commission of New South Wales, 1989.

Francis, W.D., **Australian Rainforest Trees,** Australian Government Publishing Service, 1970.

Hyland, B.P.M., **A Revision of Syzygium & Allied Genera (Myrtaceae) in Australia,** CSIRO, 1983.

Jones, D.L. & Clemesha, S.C., **Australian Ferns & Fern Allies,** Reed, 1976.

Jones, D.L. & Gray, B., **Australian Climbing Plants,** Reed, 1977.

Leiper, G., **Mutooroo Plant Use by Australian Aboriginal People,** G., Leiper.

Rotherham, E.R., Briggs, B.C., Blaxell, D.F. & Carolin, R.C., **Flowers & Plants of New South Wales and Southern Queensland,** Reed, 1982.

Society for Growing Australian Plants, **A Horticultural Guide to Australian Plant**

Webb, L.J., **Guide to the Medicinal & Poisonous Plants of Queensland,** CSIRO, 1

Williams, J.B., Harden, G.J., & McDonald, W.J.F., **Trees and Shrubs in Rainforests of New South Wales & Southern Queensland,** University of New England, 1

Williams, K.A.W., **Native Plants of Queensland, Vols. 1 & 2,** Keith Williams, 197

Wrigley, W. & Fagg, M., **Australian Native Plants,** Collins, 1979.

Stream Lily (Page 38)

# Index of Common names